SAM SHEPARD

• *Heartless* •

Sam Shepard is the Pulitzer Prize–winning author of more than forty-five plays. As an actor, he has appeared in more than thirty films, receiving an Oscar nomination in 1984 for *The Right Stuff*. He was a finalist for the W. H. Smith Literary Award for his story collection *Great Dream of Heaven*. He lives in New York and Kentucky.

• Heartless •

S A M   S H E P A R D

· *Heartless* ·

A PLAY

VINTAGE BOOKS

A DIVISION OF RANDOM HOUSE LLC

NEW YORK

A VINTAGE BOOKS ORIGINAL, SEPTEMBER 2013

Copyright © 2013 by Sam Shepard

All rights reserved. Published in the United States by Vintage Books,
a division of Random House, Inc., New York, and in Canada by
Random House of Canada Limited, Toronto.

Vintage and colophon are registered trademarks of Random House, Inc.

Library of Congress Cataloging-in-Publication Data:
Shepard, Sam.
[Plays. Selections]
Heartless : a play / By Sam Shepard.
pages   cm
ISBN 978-0-345-80680-2 (pbk.)—ISBN 978-0-345-80682-6 (ebook)
1. Ghost plays   I. Title.
PS3569.H394 H47 2013
812'.54—dc23

www.vintagebooks.com

Printed in the United States of America
10   9   8   7   6   5   4   3   2   1

Many thanks to:

Santa Fe Institute

Sylvia Plath

César Aira

Matthew Warchus

Jim Houghton

and

Peter Brook

• *Heartless* •

The world premiere of *Heartless* was produced by Signature Theatre, New York City (James Houghton, Founding Artistic Director; Erika Mallin, Executive Director; Beth Whitaker, Associate Artistic Director), and opened on August 27, 2012. It was directed by Daniel Aukin; the set design was by Eugene Lee; the costume design was by Kaye Voyce; the lighting design was by Tyler Micoleau; the sound design was by Eric Shimelonis; and the production stage manager was Donald Fried. The original cast was as follows:

SALLY	Julianne Nicholson
ROSCOE	Gary Cole
LUCY	Jenny Bacon
MABLE MURPHY	Lois Smith
ELIZABETH	Betty Gilpin

What moment in the gradual decay
Does resurrection choose? What year? What day?

— VLADIMIR NABOKOV

Everything does indeed seem to me to be shadow and
evanescence. My head spins with anguish. Really, that is
the world: a desert of fading shadows.

— EUGENE IONESCO

Act One

All stage directions are from the actor's POV toward audience. Simple set—black surround—bare-stage feel except for some stark furniture: single bed mid-stage left, placed horizontal; foot of bed facing stage left. Another single bed mid-stage right, placed vertically to audience; head of bed facing upstage. Between the beds, downstage center, is a round glass-topped table with two white metal patio chairs placed opposite each other, on either side of the table, left and right. The sense of the set is that it's essentially an outdoor patio with the two beds receding into nebulous interior territory. The whole visual arrangement is framed by tall palm trees. Extreme downstage left, looming out into the audience like a ship's prow, is a raised "lookout point" that drops off clifflike into a black void. The upstage area sweeps slightly uphill, then drops off radically into another black void. The extreme upstage edge is raised high enough so that actors can leap off it and disappear into some sort of unseen netting or, conversely, make sudden appearances into the playing area.

As lights go to black, a woman's (MABLE's) piercing voice is heard screaming someone's name.

MABLE'S VOICE: (*Screaming, offstage right.*) ELIZABETH!!!

(*Lights snap up bright. Two figures appear.* ROSCOE, *a man, mid-sixties, sits up fast in the stage right bed, facing the audience. At the same time, in stage left bed,* SALLY, *a woman in her early thirties, rolls over so her back is to audience, wrapping herself tightly in a sheet, mummy style. Pause.* ROSCOE *gets out of his bed quickly and stands, facing* SALLY's *bed. He wears green boxer shorts, a plain white T-shirt, and white socks.*)

ROSCOE: (*Disoriented.*) Sally?

(ROSCOE *moves slightly toward her bed, then stops.*)

SALLY: (*Keeping her back to audience.*) I'm sleeping.

ROSCOE: Did you scream?

SALLY: No.

ROSCOE: I thought I heard a scream.

SALLY: Go walk your dog.

(ROSCOE *turns, moves toward stage right — stops — turns back toward* SALLY, *confused.*)

ROSCOE: When I woke up I couldn't figure out where the windows were. I thought I was still in some motel somewhere—

SALLY: (*Without turning.*) You were mistaken.

(ROSCOE *turns again and exits stage right.* SALLY *immediately rolls toward audience on* ROSCOE's *exit. She sits up in her bed, naked from waist up. A long surgical scar snakes down from between her collarbones to her navel— bright pink and very prominent. She looks around the space and toward stage right, then stands, wearing white underwear, grabs a gray linen blouse, throws it on, buttons it partially while crossing downstage to stage left chair at table. She sits in chair, facing audience directly, pulls her legs up, wrapping her arms around her shins, and stares out across audience, as though seeing something in distance. Pause. Then the voice of* ROSCOE *offstage right, speaking to his dog in high-pitched falsetto. No sounds of dog whatever.* SALLY *just listens—looks out over audience.*)

ROSCOE'S VOICE: (*To dog—off right.*) Shall we take a walk? What do you think? A little walk? Piss and poop? Tinkle, tinkle. Yes? Shall we go? Oh—happy dog! Happy, happy, happy dog! Here we go! Poop and piss! Jumping, jumping! Happy, happy, happy, happy dog! Let's go—here we go! Yes—happy, happy, happy, happy—

(ROSCOE's *voice fades away off right. Pause.* SALLY *just sits and stares out in the same posture. She speaks calmly to some invisible partner in same direction as audience.*)

SALLY: You should've told me it was going to be like this. You could've warned me. 'Course, how would you know? You were the same as me. Right? Young. Babies, really. What were we then—ten? Eleven? I forget. How could we know what was up ahead? (*Pause.*) I'm glad you're still around, though—some part of you. I'm glad— (*Stops.*) You have to stop visiting me, though, in the middle of the night. I can't— I have to get some sleep. You understand? Some peace. I can't be dealing with—

(LUCY, SALLY's *older sister, enters from stage left.* LUCY *is dressed very drably in a dark cardigan sweater, a knee-length skirt, and flat shoes. She carries a metal tray in both hands with syringes, bottles, cotton balls, alcohol, etc.* LUCY *stops when she sees* SALLY *sitting there.* SALLY *ignores her, keeps staring out.*)

LUCY: You're up early.

(SALLY *holds posture, ignores her.*)

Have you taken your pills, "Sunshine"?

(*No response from* SALLY.)

Did you have your orange juice? Vitamin D?

(*No response from* SALLY.)

Sally, what are we going to do with you?

SALLY: (*Holding posture.*) Who's "we"?

(LUCY *exhales, crosses to table, sets down medicine tray, and sits in opposite chair, stage right.* SALLY *remains standing still, staring straight ahead.* LUCY *goes about her daily routine of filling syringes with various serums, medicines—flicking the bottles expertly as she speaks to* SALLY.)

LUCY: (*As she works.*) Did you do anything domestic this morning—like make coffee, flip an egg—?

(SALLY *shakes her head.*)

How 'bout your new friend—what's his name?

SALLY: Roscoe.

LUCY: How 'bout Roscoe. He looks like the "rise and shine" type. Did Roscoe put any coffee on?

(SALLY *hunches her shoulders.*)

I can smell something warm and nutty—

SALLY: Must've, then.

LUCY: We're just sociable as hell this morning, aren't we?

SALLY: Oh—sorry.

LUCY: Don't apologize.

(*Long pause.* SALLY *remains in her posture,* LUCY *continues her work.*)

Did you happen to hear a scream, earlier?

(SALLY *slowly turns her head toward* LUCY *and stares at her.*)

SALLY: What?

LUCY: A scream. High-pitched—piercing. Nightmarish.

(SALLY *turns away from her, back to original posture.*)

SALLY: Must've been Mable.

LUCY: Mom doesn't scream. She moans.

SALLY: She used to scream.

LUCY: That was way back.

SALLY: Yeah—she's been screaming for decades.

LUCY: I wouldn't say that, exactly.

SALLY: What would you say?

LUCY: Well—of course she screamed back when she fell out of that tree.

SALLY: Yeah.

LUCY: But that was a long time ago when Whitmore left her. You weren't even around.

SALLY: I was here. Right here. When you brought her back in pieces. She was screaming then.

LUCY: Well—she was in terrible pain.

SALLY: The police came to the door.

LUCY: I don't remember that.

SALLY: Of course you don't.

(*Long pause where the two of them just sit there in silence.*)

What?

LUCY: Screaming, I mean.

SALLY: Screaming neighbors.

LUCY: Domestic dispute or something.

SALLY: I've never seen the neighbors, have you?

LUCY: Once.

SALLY: I've seen their cars. Their gardeners.

LUCY: Who could've been screaming, then?

SALLY: This is L.A. People scream all the time.

(*Long pause.*)

LUCY: What happened to your friend? "Boscoe," was it?

SALLY: Roscoe.

LUCY: Whatever.

SALLY: No. Not "whatever." That's his name—Roscoe. How would you like it if somebody called you "Juicy" instead of Lucy?

LUCY: Sally, for Christ's sake! It's so much fun trying to have a conversation with you!

SALLY: Fun?

LUCY: (*Short pause.*) Where is your friend—*Roscoe?* (*Exaggerating name.*)

SALLY: Walking his *dog.* (*Exaggerating "dog."*)

LUCY: (*Pause.*) Oh—he's got a dog? That changes my opinion of him.

SALLY: Why's that?

LUCY: He's the one who just recently left his wife and children, isn't he? Ran off?

SALLY: So?

LUCY: Well, he must be looking for a replacement, then.

SALLY: With the dog?

LUCY: Yes. Well—

SALLY: The dog replaces the children?

LUCY: I'm not—

SALLY: That's deep, Lucy. That's really deep. Did you just come up with that on your own?

(SALLY *gets up suddenly, crosses upstage, gets into her bed, and wraps herself up tightly in sheet, as before, then turns her back on* LUCY. LUCY *stands, gathering her tray together.*)

LUCY: Well—maybe you just need more rest, Sally. Maybe that's it. Lack of sleep can make a person crabby and irritable. Studies show— (*She begins to cross stage right, then stops.*) You really ought to take your medicine, though. You want to stay alive, don't you?

(LUCY *exits stage right.* SALLY *just lies there with her back to audience for a short while, then suddenly starts singing, a capella—in full voice, while remaining in posture, her back to audience.*)

SALLY: (*Singing.*)
I want to stay alive
I want to stay alive

How many times I catch myself
I want to stay alive
I'm slipping all the time
Falling in my mind
Ten times a day I catch myself
I want to stay alive.

(*She stops.* ROSCOE'S VOICE *dovetails in from off right.*)

ROSCOE'S VOICE: (*Calling from off right.*) Sally! Oh, Sally! You didn't go back to sleep, did you, because I've got something for you! Big gooey surprise!

(SALLY *rolls over, facing audience.*)

SALLY: What could that be?

ROSCOE'S VOICE: Jelly do-nuts!

SALLY: (*Sitting up in bed.*) Jelly do-nuts?

ROSCOE'S VOICE: Deep-fried!

SALLY: What flavor?

ROSCOE'S VOICE: Raspberry. Mango.

SALLY: Mango? In a do-nut?

ROSCOE'S VOICE: "California Exotic," they call it. Golden! Oozing!

SALLY: They must inject it or something. How do they get mango in there?

(ROSCOE *enters from down right, heading toward table, a coffee cup in each hand and a white bakery bag containing do-nuts dangling between his teeth. He crosses slowly to table, careful not to spill coffee; sets cups down and then bag of do-nuts. Sally watches closely from bed.*)

You would've made a great husband. Maybe.

ROSCOE: Ooops! Forgot the half-and-half.

(ROSCOE *turns and darts back off right.* SALLY *leaps out of bed, goes to table, and peeks into bag, sniffing do-nuts, then crumples it back up again. She sits in stage left chair again, picks up coffee and slurps it.* ROSCOE *reenters from down right with half-and-half, plates, and napkins, talking as he enters.*)

I myself am a huge fan of the jelly do-nut. Going way back to my junkie days. Avenue D, Fourteenth Street, Dunkin' Donuts, cops, transvestite fistfights, hookers, and faggots—the strung out and hopeless.

SALLY: What a list.

(ROSCOE *sits at table, puts do-nuts on plates, distributes napkins, etc., while* SALLY *slurps coffee and listens.*)

ROSCOE: Everyone had an appetite for the juicy jelly do-nut. It was a religion.

SALLY: It gave them hope.

ROSCOE: It did.

SALLY: They began to believe in themselves.

ROSCOE: Renewed faith.

(*Pause.*)

SALLY: You were a junkie?

ROSCOE: Weren't we all?

SALLY: Well—it's hard to picture.

ROSCOE: Sixties—you know.

SALLY: I wasn't born until '82.

ROSCOE: Poor you.

SALLY: Why? What'd I miss?

ROSCOE: All the assassinations. (*About do-nuts.*) I think I'll cut these in half. They're huge.

SALLY: Busy, busy, busy.

(ROSCOE *gets up and exits—again stage right.* SALLY *immediately picks up a do-nut, smells it, then licks a gob of the filling off it. When* ROSCOE *reenters with a butter knife she quickly puts do-nut back on plate.* ROSCOE *sits and starts cutting do-nuts in half.*)

Don't you think I should be taping this? Seems like an opportunity.

ROSCOE: (*Cutting do-nuts.*) What?

SALLY: All this—activity. This—spontaneous life. For the documentary.

ROSCOE: I hate documentaries.

SALLY: No, I mean—the film—what we've been working on—whatever you want to call it.

ROSCOE: Pretending to be real life.

SALLY: There's no pretending.

ROSCOE: Suit yourself.

(SALLY *rushes upstage to her bed and hauls a video camera and equipment out from underneath it. She puts on earphones, fastens the battery pack around her waist, adjusts focus, etc. She returns to table hoisting camera on her shoulder, starts shooting* ROSCOE *eating do-nut, drinking coffee.*)

(*Directly to camera.*) This is me in the act of devouring a lemon-filled jelly do-nut. "Jelly" is a bit of a misnomer in this case since it seems to be actually a kind of custard—meringue, maybe.

SALLY: (*Still shooting.*) Professor Hubbard—uh, could you give us any insight into the comparisons between Cervantes and say, oh, a contemporary Latin American writer such as—César Aira?

ROSCOE: *An Episode in the Life of a Landscape Painter?*

SALLY: That's the one.

ROSCOE: Well, the only valid comparison I could make is the adventure itself—two men, horseback, trekking out into the vast unknown, in search of romance.

SALLY: (*Still shooting.*) Romance?

ROSCOE: Meaning.

SALLY: Meaning?

ROSCOE: Stop repeating everything I say!

SALLY (*Eye to camera.*) We're shooting, you know. We're taping this.

ROSCOE: I know, I know. But it's boring when you do that.

SALLY: What's boring?

ROSCOE: Repeating everything! It's boring.

SALLY: (*Still shooting.*) Isn't repetition part of primitive ritual?

ROSCOE: (*Throws down do-nut.*) Oh my God.

SALLY: Well—isn't it? Poetry—song—dance—the drum—

ROSCOE: Can we move on to something—

SALLY: All right, all right. So touchy all of a sudden.

ROSCOE: I'm not touchy!

SALLY: You are.

(SALLY *moves in circles around* ROSCOE, *in and out, getting different angles with the camera.*)

ROSCOE: I'm not touchy! I just don't know if this film idea is—

SALLY: Let's change the subject, then.

ROSCOE: Let's.

SALLY: What's all this "junkie" business, for instance? First I've heard about it. Shocking, actually. From heroin to scholarship?

ROSCOE: It's not a "business"—well—I guess it is.

SALLY: Quite lucrative.

ROSCOE: That's not what I was—

SALLY: Tell us about the "time"—the era—you know—the street life.

ROSCOE: I liked it better when we were just—exchanging pleasantries. You know—the camera changes everything.

SALLY: (*Still shooting.*) How?

ROSCOE: I don't know. It stops something.

SALLY: Forget about the camera.

ROSCOE: I can't!

SALLY: What about you leaving your wife and family? There's a subject.

ROSCOE: I don't want to talk about that.

SALLY: (*Taking camera down from her shoulder.*) You're so grouchy all of a sudden.

ROSCOE: I'm sorry—I—I just feel like—I'd just like to have some coffee and—eat a jelly do-nut and—not think about anything.

SALLY: Fine by me.

(SALLY *sets camera on floor, under table, takes earphones off, sits back down opposite* ROSCOE, *in stage left chair, and slurps coffee. Pause.*)

ROSCOE: How's your mother?

SALLY: What?

ROSCOE: Your mother?

SALLY: Haven't checked. That's not my job. It's Lucy's. Juicy Lucy.

ROSCOE: I see.

SALLY: Lucy's in there right now—shooting her up. Why don't you ask her?

ROSCOE: We're on a junkie jag here, aren't we?

SALLY: You started it. Sedatives—vitamins—antibiotics— I don't know. A regular chemical cocktail.

ROSCOE: Right.

SALLY: She's got a nurse with her as well.

ROSCOE: Can't the nurse—?

SALLY: My mother has quirky requirements.

ROSCOE: What's the matter with her?

SALLY: Nobody seems to know.

ROSCOE: Doctors?

SALLY: "Rigors," they're calling it.

ROSCOE: Oh—so they have a name for it?

SALLY: Psychosomatic.

ROSCOE: Soon as they have a name they give up.

SALLY: What?

ROSCOE: Trying to figure out what it is.

SALLY: Paralysis—her hands are like claws. Feet all seized up.

ROSCOE: What happened to her? Something must've happened.

SALLY: Fell out of a pine tree. Way back.

ROSCOE: Pine tree?

SALLY: Middle of the night. High up.

ROSCOE: Climbing? What was she doing?

SALLY: Accident. Trauma—you know.

ROSCOE: Do you think I could meet her?

SALLY: Why?

ROSCOE: Well—I'd just like to meet her. We're all living in the same house.

SALLY: I thought you said you were just visiting. On the mend.

ROSCOE: Well, sure—yeah.

SALLY: Just to heal up from your separation. That's what you told me, isn't it?

ROSCOE: That's right. Don't think I'm not grateful for the hospitality.

SALLY: You're not "living" here.

ROSCOE: No.

SALLY: This isn't your home.

ROSCOE: No, it isn't.

SALLY: You're a visitor.

ROSCOE: Yes!

SALLY: Good.

(*Long pause.* ROSCOE *gazes out over the audience to the distance.*)

ROSCOE: How did you find this place, anyway?

SALLY: My mother's owned it for years. Divorce settlement.

ROSCOE: Spectacular view.

SALLY: (*Looking out in same direction.*) Yeah. They say James Dean used to stay here.

ROSCOE: Really?

SALLY: When he was first starting out. Yeah. Slept in that same bed you're sleeping in. Just like George Washington.

ROSCOE: You're kidding!

SALLY: I never "kid."

ROSCOE: That's unbelievable! James Dean?

SALLY: Yeah. Fresh out of Indiana. 'Course it might be just another fable in the L.A. canon of hysterical imaginings.

ROSCOE: Hysterical what?

SALLY: Never mind.

(*Long pause. They both stare out over audience in the direction of the great Los Angeles Valley.*)

ROSCOE: (*Staring out.*) I've never seen it from way up like this. You can see the whole valley.

SALLY: Yeah. The whole nasty panorama in one gasping breath. When it's clear, you can see the Pacific.

ROSCOE: (*Pointing*) Is that it?

SALLY: What?

ROSCOE: That bluish band way out there.

SALLY: (*Looking where he's pointing.*) No, that's smog. It's over there—when you can see it. The ocean. (*Pointing in different direction.*)

ROSCOE: Blue smog? I thought smog was yellow.

SALLY: Changes color with the seasons. Like leaves back East.

ROSCOE: (*Staring out.*) You know, the Spanish recorded smog in their journals as far back as the 1500s.

SALLY: What color was it then, Professor?

(LUCY *enters from stage right with metal tray, empty bottles, etc. She stops when she sees* ROSCOE.)

LUCY: Oh—looks like you're back.

(ROSCOE, *very gentlemanly, stands, extends his hand.*)

ROSCOE: Yes—Roscoe Hubbard, and—you must be Lucy?

LUCY: (*Setting down tray and shaking* ROSCOE's *hand.*) The sister, that's right. Lucy, the sister.

SALLY: I'm glad we all know each other now.

LUCY: How was the dog walk?

ROSCOE: Fine. Just fine. Lovely roads up here. Smell of eucalyptus. Mockingbirds—mocking.

SALLY: Pit bulls. Razor wire.

(*Pause.*)

ROSCOE: (*To* LUCY.) Well—would you like some coffee? We're just—

LUCY: Love some. Thank you.

(ROSCOE *exits stage right.* LUCY *sits in* ROSCOE's *chair. She and* SALLY *sit in silence.* SALLY *slurps her coffee.* LUCY *stares out over L.A. Long pause.*)

SALLY: That's *his* chair, you know.

LUCY: Oh— (*She stands abruptly, looks at chair.*) I didn't realize they were designated.

SALLY: He was sitting there.

LUCY: (*Looking around for another chair.*) Right. Well, there must be another one.

SALLY: Must be.

(*Long pause.* SALLY *slurps coffee.* LUCY *remains standing.*)

How's the matriarch this morning?

LUCY: (*Stays standing.*) Same.

SALLY: Talking?

LUCY: Some.

SALLY: Coherent?

LUCY: In and out.

SALLY: Awake, though?

LUCY: Apparently.

SALLY: (*Short pause.*) What's she talk about these days?

LUCY: She told me she heard a scream. Same time as me.

SALLY: In her dream.

LUCY: Somebody's name.

(ROSCOE *enters from right with a cup of coffee and a light folding chair.*)

ROSCOE: Here we go! Had to find a chair.

LUCY: Oh—you brought a chair. How nice.

ROSCOE: Yes. You sit in mine and I'll use this one.

LUCY: Oh, that's all right.

ROSCOE: I insist.

(ROSCOE *sets coffee down for* LUCY, *then unfolds chair and places it upstage center of table and sits between women.*)

SALLY: This is kinda like an old black-and-white movie. Everybody's so polite.

LUCY: (*Sitting; leaning toward do-nuts.*) Are these—? (*She picks one up.*)

ROSCOE: Jelly do-nuts? Yes, they are.

SALLY: The real deal.

ROSCOE: You're more than welcome to have one. Your sister doesn't seem to—

(SALLY *grabs a do-nut and shoves the whole thing in her mouth.* LUCY *and* ROSCOE *watch as she munches away.*)

LUCY: (*To* SALLY.) Good?

SALLY: (*Mouth full.*) Delicious.

(*Pause as* SALLY *chews.*)

ROSCOE: (*To* LUCY.) I was hoping to meet your mother but Sally doesn't—

SALLY: (*Chewing.*) What?

ROSCOE: Well—didn't you say that—

SALLY: (*Chewing.*) I don't care if you meet her. Why should I care?

ROSCOE: I thought you said—

LUCY: I don't think it's a good idea.

SALLY: Why not?

LUCY: Because she's—

SALLY: What?

LUCY: Compromised. (*To* ROSCOE.) You understand—

ROSCOE: Compromised?

LUCY: Diminished?

ROSCOE: Oh—

LUCY: Not herself.

ROSCOE: Well, none of us—

(SALLY *pulls rest of uneaten do-nut out of her mouth and plops it on table.*)

SALLY: It's all an act.

LUCY: (*To* ROSCOE.) She's not ready to meet anyone just yet. Let's put it that way.

SALLY: Pumped full of drugs, is what it is.

LUCY: That's not entirely true, Sally.

SALLY: She doesn't know Monday morning from Friday night.

ROSCOE: Drugs?

SALLY: "Painkillers." In the modern vernacular.

LUCY: My sister's exaggerating.

SALLY: Ha!

(*Pause.* LUCY *shifts position in her chair and accidentally kicks* SALLY's *video equipment under table.* LUCY *looks under table.*)

LUCY: What's all this?

SALLY: My stuff.

LUCY: Camera?

SALLY: Yeah.

LUCY: What for?

SALLY: We're making a little movie—Roscoe and me.

LUCY: Oh—what about?

SALLY: Has it got to be "about" something?

LUCY: Well—usually there's a theme.

SALLY: It's about Roscoe.

LUCY: Oh—

SALLY: His life—his career—

LUCY: Oh, I didn't realize—

ROSCOE: I don't really have a career.

LUCY: I didn't realize you were so interesting.

ROSCOE: No, I know—I don't appear to be, do I?

SALLY: He's multifaceted. Chaotic.

LUCY: Really? (*To* ROSCOE.) Well, what is it that you do?

SALLY: He's famous.

LUCY: Is that right? I've never heard of you. What's your name again?

SALLY: Roscoe Hubbard.

ROSCOE: Well, no—fame isn't exactly the right—

SALLY: "Infamous"—a scholar—professor—

LUCY: What do you teach?

ROSCOE: Cervantes, mostly.

LUCY: What?

ROSCOE: *Don Quixote*.

LUCY: Oh.

ROSCOE: Borges, also.

LUCY: How do you say it?

ROSCOE: (*Overenunciating.*) Bor-ges. You put a little "h" sound into the "g." A little exhale.

LUCY: (*Tries it, fails.*) "Boor-geese."

ROSCOE: Excellent.

SALLY: What do you mean? It's really shitty. It's not "excellent."

LUCY: (*Tries again, fails.*) "Bore-gaaze."

SALLY: Just knock it off!

ROSCOE: (*To* SALLY.) No—she's—

SALLY: She's butchering it! One of your favorite authors and she's making hash of it.

LUCY: All right—I just thought I'd give it a whirl.

ROSCOE: I was impressed. For a first effort it was—

SALLY: It was really shitty. Didn't even resemble the man's name.

LUCY: (*To* ROSCOE.) Well, I'm very sorry I haven't heard of you until just now.

ROSCOE: No, no—don't be sorry. That's quite all right.

LUCY: What other things have you done?

SALLY: He was a junkie, once.

(*Long dead pause.*)

ROSCOE: I wasn't really—

(LUCY *stands, collecting her tray.*)

SALLY: You were. You told me you were.

ROSCOE: It was a figure— (*To* LUCY.) Would you like some more coffee?

LUCY: (*Standing.*) I don't think so—no.

SALLY: He came up in the age of heroin—beatniks— Burroughs and Corso.

LUCY: How sad.

ROSCOE: (*Offering do-nuts to* LUCY.) Jelly do-nut?

LUCY: Thank you, no.

ROSCOE: Nice meeting you.

LUCY: Likewise.

(LUCY *exits stage left, with tray. Long pause.* SALLY *slurps her coffee.* ROSCOE *looks out over Los Angeles.*)

ROSCOE: Thanks.

SALLY: You told me you were a junkie.

ROSCOE: I snorted a little! I never actually developed a "jones." It was a figure of speech.

SALLY: A what?

ROSCOE: A figure of speech!

SALLY: No—the other. "Jones"?

ROSCOE: A habit.

SALLY: Oh—you left that part out.

ROSCOE: I was just—talking through my hat.

SALLY: Bragging? About being a junkie?

ROSCOE: To give you a kind of—impression.

SALLY: But we've already—

ROSCOE: Not for that reason.

SALLY: What, then?

ROSCOE: Just—to make you think I was someone with experience.

SALLY: Experience? Like Jimi Hendrix?

ROSCOE: No! Not just another—"academic."

SALLY: Oh. (*Pause.*) So it turns out you're a liar, then. A pretender.

ROSCOE: No, no—I really did live through all that.

SALLY: All what?

ROSCOE: All that—Sixties stuff: mattress on the floor— cockroach across your feet—nickel bags half filled with oregano—

SALLY: You lie about everything, don't you?

ROSCOE: No! But you don't have to tell your sister I'm a—

SALLY: You're lying right now.

ROSCOE: I'm not lying!!

SALLY: I can tell. I can see it in your eyes. No wonder your wife left you.

(SALLY *gets up, goes to her bed, and flops down on it—lies on her back, staring at ceiling.*)

ROSCOE: She didn't leave me. I left *her*!

(*Long pause.* SALLY *just stares at ceiling.* ROSCOE *stares at floor—silent.*)

SALLY: Doesn't matter.

ROSCOE: It does! If you think everything I say is a lie.

SALLY: It's not what you "say."

ROSCOE: What is it, then?

SALLY: What you don't say.

ROSCOE: I'm not following you.

(*Long pause.*)

SALLY: You should go back to her. It's such a waste.

ROSCOE: What is?

SALLY: Time. You—running up and down the highway like some headless chicken. What do you think you're supposed to be doing?

ROSCOE: I don't know.

SALLY: "Being free" or something? Being your own person? What're you trying to prove, Professor?

ROSCOE: Nothing—I guess.

SALLY: You should go back.

ROSCOE: It's too late.

SALLY: How long were you together?

ROSCOE: Long.

SALLY: Then it can't be too late.

ROSCOE: What is this sudden empathy with my wife, for God's sake? Some feminine manifesto, out of the blue?

You don't know my wife! You don't know what she's feeling. You've never even met her!

(*Suddenly* MABLE MURPHY, *the mother of* SALLY *and* LUCY, *is rolled on stage right in a wheelchair being pushed by* ELIZABETH—*a tall, elegant, beautiful young nurse.* MABLE *has a blue plaid blanket draped over her lap and a dark green shawl around her neck. She is in her late seventies; her hands are seized up and clutched to her chest like claws, her feet twisted up.* ELIZABETH *is completely dressed in white, classic nurse style, including cap, low-heeled shoes, white stockings, starched skirt.* ELIZABETH *brings the wheelchair to an abrupt halt.* SALLY *immediately sits up in her bed.* ROSCOE *stands.*)

SALLY: Mom!

MABLE: Put some clothes on. What is this—a burlesque show?

SALLY: What're you doing up, Mom?

MABLE: (*To* ROSCOE.) Who're you?

ROSCOE: Uh—

SALLY: This is my friend—Roscoe.

MABLE: Let him speak for himself. He can speak for himself— (*To* ROSCOE.) Can't you?

ROSCOE: Yes, ma'am.

MABLE: Well, then?

ROSCOE: I'm—

MABLE: What kind of "friend" do you call yourself, Roscoe? A "friend friend," a "casual friend," or a "friend to the death"? Are you any of those?

ROSCOE: Well—me and Sally—

SALLY: We're working on a project together, Mom.

MABLE: Put some clothes on! What's the matter with you? Has the partition between private and public become completely obliterated?

(SALLY *jumps up and starts digging around under the blankets; pulls out a pair of blue pajama bottoms and puts them on quickly.*)

Where do you come from, Roscoe? What neck of the woods? So rare that we have a houseguest.

ROSCOE: Kentucky, ma'am.

MABLE: Ah yes—bourbon and horses.

ROSCOE: Yes, ma'am. That's right.

MABLE: They say it's the water.

ROSCOE: What?

MABLE: Limestone. Filtered through limestone. The water.

ROSCOE: Oh—yes. That's right.

MABLE: Born and raised?

ROSCOE: What?

MABLE: In Kentucky?

ROSCOE: No, ma'am. My dad was in the air force.

MABLE: What's that mean? Airplanes?

ROSCOE: No—town to town. You know—

MABLE: Rootless.

ROSCOE: Yes, ma'am.

MABLE: Stop calling me "ma'am" all the time. Feels like we're in "Gone With the Goddamn Wind."

ROSCOE: Sorry.

MABLE: And don't apologize either. I don't subscribe to the cult of apology. Sin is sin. It's guilt we're trying to squirm out of.

ROSCOE: Right.

MABLE: Never could stomach a slinking dog with its tail sucked up between its legs.

ROSCOE: No.

MABLE: Trembling and whimpering.

ROSCOE: Right.

MABLE: Makes you want to kick it.

(*Pause.* ROSCOE *looks to* SALLY.)

ROSCOE: It's so nice to finally—

MABLE: You're kinda old to be messing around with my daughter, aren't you?

SALLY: Mom—

ROSCOE: Ma'am—I wasn't—

MABLE: I just told you about that "ma'am" stuff, didn't I?

ROSCOE: Sorry—

MABLE: (*Turns away from* ROSCOE.) Oh, Jesus—another creature of habit. (*Turns back to him.*) How old are you, anyway, "Roscoe"—

ROSCOE: Sixty-five.

MABLE: Sixty-five. That's more'n twice her age. You oughta be ashamed but you're not, are you? You're probably secretly proud.

ROSCOE: We're just—

MABLE: Don't bullshit me, mister! I can tell when something's going on. She wouldn't be standin' around half naked if something wasn't going on.

SALLY: I'm not staying here for this!

(SALLY *storms off stage left, cinching up her pajama bottoms. Pause.*)

MABLE: (*Looking stage left.*) Flighty. (*Pause. She turns to* ROSCOE.) Why don't you sit down? You're making me nervous, "Roscoe."

(ROSCOE *sits.*)

(*Signaling* LIZ *with a wag of her head.*) 'Lizabeth!

(LIZ *knows intuitively where* MABLE *wants to be and wheels her over to table; stops upstage center of table, facing audience.* ROSCOE *keeps a fascinated eye on* LIZ.)

You can have a seat if you've a mind to, Liz. Take a load off.

(LIZ *applies hand brake on wheelchair, then sits in stage left chair across from* ROSCOE, *who continues to stare at her.* LIZ *folds her hands in her lap, legs together, very proper. She smiles sheepishly at* ROSCOE. MABLE *leans forward over table and sees wad of chewed-up donut that* SALLY *had spit out on table.*)

What's this mess? Vomit on my table?

ROSCOE: Oh, that's just—

(LIZ *stands quickly—picks up wad of do-nut with napkin.*)

MABLE: Throw that to the squirrels, Liz. They'll devour it. Nasty, disease-ridden creatures. Remnants of the plague, I reckon.

ROSCOE: Plague?

(LIZ *takes do-nut mess in napkin, crosses upstage center, and tosses it over cliff—extreme upstage edge. She returns to table, rubbing her hands together.*)

MABLE: My ex-husband, Whitmore, used to shoot them from the porch with a .410. Provided him with miles of entertainment. Before the days of television, of course—video games—pornography. No—that's been around, hasn't it? Haven't they recently discovered ancient cave drawings of genitalia?

(ROSCOE *keeps his eyes riveted on* LIZ *as she sits again at table, across from him, picks up fresh napkin, and cleans her fingers.* MABLE *sees* ROSCOE's *fixation on* LIZ. *To* ROSCOE.)

Oh—this is my personal nurse, Elizabeth Bynon. She's gone mute for some reason but she's loyal to a fault. Aren't you, Liz?

(LIZ *nods, smiles at* ROSCOE, *and continues cleaning her hands.*)

She's from Newcastle, England, where they make the brown ale that'll put you in the nuthouse if you're not careful. She's a Geordie. Had a lovely, lilting accent when I first met her—something Swedish about it— Scandinavian. But then something happened—didn't it, Liz?

(*Pause.* MABLE *looks to* LIZ *for an answer, but* LIZ *just stares at* ROSCOE.)

What *did* happen, Liz?

(LIZ *just shrugs; smiles at* ROSCOE.)

Anyway, something must've happened, we're not sure what, and she clammed up altogether. Hasn't affected her loyalty, though, or her steadfastness. Not one iota. Throw herself in front of a freight train for me. Wouldn't you, Liz? If need be.

(LIZ *keeps wiping her hands, smiling at* ROSCOE.)

That's what we're all looking for, isn't it, Roscoe? Unconditional loyalty. When you come right down to it. That's what we secretly pray for, day in and day out. Don't you think? Absolute forgiveness.

ROSCOE: Yes ma'a— (*Stops himself.*)

MABLE: Someone blind to all our faults. Who only sees the angel in us—the benevolent creature. Mothers, for instance. (*To* ROSCOE.) Don't you think? Wouldn't you say so?

ROSCOE: Mothers?

MABLE: Absolutely. Toward their children—their own kind. Unconditional love. Not fathers so much— fathers are a whole different bag of worms.

ROSCOE: I suppose so.

MABLE: Wouldn't you agree with that, Liz? About fathers?

(LIZ *nods, smiles at* ROSCOE.)

Fathers make impossible demands. Expectations, then disappointments. One's the product of the other. A snake biting its own tail.

ROSCOE: Yes—I mean—

MABLE: You could be a cold-blooded killer and your mother would forgive you.

ROSCOE: Me?

MABLE: Slaughter innocent bystanders in broad daylight. Decapitate infants with a bowie knife. Slice open their tender bowels—pull out their purple squirming intestines and eat them raw. Your mother would forgive you.

ROSCOE: *My* mother?

MABLE: She would. No question. Wouldn't she, Liz?

(LIZ *nods, giggles, and smiles at* ROSCOE.)

Not the father, though. No. The father would be full of judgment and condemnation. Contempt. He would be the prosecutor—the hangman, divorcing himself entirely from all blood connection. He would disown you.

ROSCOE: The father?

MABLE: Absolutely. Then, of course, there's the whole question of lust. Isn't there?

ROSCOE: (*Standing suddenly.*) Lust?

MABLE: Sit down. We're just getting started.

(ROSCOE *sits again.*)

We can't sweep lust under the table.

ROSCOE: No.

MABLE: No. Can't be simply disregarded. We're all human, don't you think?

ROSCOE: Human? Sure.

MABLE: That's right. Much as we'd like to get away from it.

ROSCOE: Well—what else would we be? I mean—

MABLE: Demons—dragons—banshees—there's a whole list. Goes on forever.

ROSCOE: Oh—well—yes—but those aren't—

MABLE: What?

ROSCOE: Human.

MABLE: No. But they're not without some substance, are they?

ROSCOE: Well—

MABLE: How does Shakespeare put it?

ROSCOE: Shakespeare?

MABLE: About lust. The power of lust. (*Suddenly quoting.*)

> *. . . a waste of shame*
> *Is lust in action; and till action, lust*
> *Is perjured, murderous, bloody, full of blame . . .*

Isn't that the way it goes?

ROSCOE: All I know is Cervantes. I'm not—

MABLE: Isn't it, Liz?

(LIZ *nods, keeps smiling at* ROSCOE.)

Brush up on your Shakespeare, Roscoe. We only have this one life to live. Can't be lazy, can we?

ROSCOE: Well, Shakespeare isn't my area of—

MABLE: It's coming back to me now. (*Quoting again.*)

> *All this the world well knows; yet none knows well*
> *To shun the heaven that leads men to this hell.*

That's it! That's it, isn't it? The mind's such a marvelous muscle! There it was—just laying around like a sleeping cat, waiting for me to come along and kick its furry ass! "To shun the heaven that leads men to this hell." Isn't that just the most gorgeous thing you ever heard?

(*Long pause.* MABLE *looks back and forth between* ROS- COE *and* LIZ *for a response.*)

Liz?

(LIZ *just smiles at* ROSCOE, *who grows more nervous.*)

Liz?

ROSCOE: (*To* MABLE.) I happen to have a pot of coffee on the stove in there, and—

MABLE: I was onto something here!

ROSCOE: I just thought you might like to take a break, Mrs.—?

MABLE: Murphy. Mable Murphy. County Cork, originally. Not me, of course, but those on the other side of the grass.

ROSCOE: Cup of coffee, Mrs. Murphy?

MABLE: Do I look like someone who could handle a cup of coffee?

ROSCOE: Well—um—I think we might have some straws.

MABLE: Straws?

ROSCOE: Long ones. I think I saw some.

(MABLE *looks to* LIZ, *perplexed.*)

MABLE: (*To* LIZ.) Long straws? For coffee?

(LIZ *shrugs.*)

Wouldn't they just melt? Liz?

(LIZ *shrugs again.* MABLE *turns back to* ROSCOE.)

All right. We'll give it a whirl.

ROSCOE: Great!

(ROSCOE *leaps to his feet, glad to be getting out of the situation; exits stage right. Long pause.* MABLE *stares out over the audience, toward Los Angeles.* LIZ, *hands folded, remains in chair.* MABLE *nudges piece of jelly do-nut with her elbow, examines it.*)

MABLE: (*Smirking.*) Straws. (*Looking out toward L.A. She directs question to* LIZ, *who is also looking out front.*) What do you think, Liz? Total idiot?

(LIZ *shrugs her shoulders, keeps looking out.* MABLE, *too, continues looking out.*)

Psychopath?

(LIZ *squints, wrinkling her nose, and shakes her head.*)

Pedophile?

(LIZ *shakes her head.*)

Lost in the woods?

(LIZ *nods. Pause.* ROSCOE *reenters from right with another cup of steaming coffee and a long straw wrapped in white paper.*)

ROSCOE: (*Crossing to table.*) Here we go! I was right.

(ROSCOE *sets coffee down in front of* MABLE, *then holds straw up.*)

Straw! (*Smiling.*) Long straw. (*Starts unwrapping it.*)

MABLE: Let *her* do that. I don't know where your hands have been.

(ROSCOE *hands straw to* LIZ, *who takes it, smiling at* ROSCOE *all the while. She unwraps it carefully;* ROSCOE *sits back down.* MABLE *begins to ramble— as much to herself as to anyone in particular.* ROSCOE *only has eyes for* LIZ. MABLE *still looking out over L.A.*)

I suppose there have been mothers who've gone bad. When you think about it. Bad apples. Renegades. Miscreants. Got to be. Devouring their children. Stuffing them in Dumpsters. Drowning them in muddy pools under the full moon. I'd like to think they were in the minority, though. Rarest cases. What do you suppose it could've been? Revenge? Infidelity? Betrayal of one kind or another. Maybe just plain old madness. Maybe as simple as that. The call of madness.

(LIZ *puts the unwrapped straw in* MABLE's *coffee, then guides the other end to* MABLE's *lips.* MABLE *closes her eyes and sips on straw. Suddenly spitting out straw and coffee.*)

GODDAMNIT!!!

(ROSCOE *stands,* LIZ *stands, takes napkin, and tries to clean up* MABLE, *who is spitting and twitching her head from side to side.*)

ROSCOE: What is it?

MABLE: Hot!! That's what it is!

(ROSCOE *sticks his fingers in* MABLE's *cup to test heat.*)

Don't put your fingers in my coffee! Where were you raised!

ROSCOE: (*Pulling back.*) I can get some ice.

MABLE: I don't want any ice. What am I gonna do with ice? Suck on it?

ROSCOE: I'm sorry.

MABLE: Sit back down!

(ROSCOE *sits.* LIZ *keeps cleaning up.*)

Didn't want any coffee either. (*To* ROSCOE.) How'd I let you talk me into that?

ROSCOE: I just thought—

MABLE: How'd I let him put that in my head, Liz? Coffee! What a dumb idea. I hate coffee. (*To* LIZ, *who sits back down.*) You should've seen this coming. You could've warned me. Given me counsel.

(LIZ, *sitting, begins folding and unfolding napkin nervously, in her lap. She keeps her head down and seems ashamed.* MABLE *continues harangue.*)

You're the one who's supposed to save me from these predicaments. If I can't trust you, who else can I trust? Nobody. I'm vulnerable as a naked infant. Look at me!

(LIZ *takes a quick peek at* MABLE, *then drops her head again and continues with napkin.*)

ROSCOE: She didn't—

MABLE: You stay out of this!

ROSCOE: But I don't think she—

MABLE: You know nothing about us, do you? An utter stranger—waltzing into our lives as though— Who are you, anyway? Some vagabond, homeless wretch! Spawn of the air force!

ROSCOE: I just don't think you can hold her responsible for—

MABLE: It's none of your business, is it?

ROSCOE: Well, it just seems unfair to—

MABLE: Unfair! What's fairness got to do with it? None of us asked for any of this!

ROSCOE: What? No—I didn't mean—

MABLE: You shut up!

(*Silence—pause.*) "Fairness." What are you, the "morality clerk"? (*Nodding toward* LIZ, *who continues, head down, folding napkin.*)

Take a look at this beautiful young creature. Sentenced . . . (*Continuing.*) . . . to silence. Numb as a stone. Dumb as toast. Where's the fairness in that? Look at my daughter—Sally—look at her. You know about her, don't you? Or has she told you the whole story?

ROSCOE: Story?

MABLE: 'Course not. The "whole story" is something that eludes us, isn't it? Where did you two meet, anyhow? You and Sally?

(LIZ, *very quietly, begins to weep, her head still bowed, continuing to fold and unfold the napkin in her lap.* MABLE *ignores her.* ROSCOE, *keenly aware of* LIZ, *slowly stands, keeping his eyes riveted on* LIZ *as he talks to* MABLE.)

ROSCOE: (*Slowly standing.*) Uh—I'm not sure now, talk show, I think it was. She was—interviewing me about—literature—

MABLE: (*Oblivious to* LIZ, *who keeps sobbing.*) Talk show—interview—of course—that's where everyone meets these days, isn't it? Talk shows—"reality shows"—tango contests—Facebook. The boredom is epidemic. Should never have raised her up in this godforsaken wasteland.

(LIZ *weeps slightly louder—*ROSCOE *makes a little move toward her, then stops himself.*)

Should've raised her in Nebraska—like Liz here. Sand Hills—salt of the earth. You don't see Liz prancing around in her bra and panties. Do you? No, sir.

(LIZ *keeps crying.*)

ROSCOE: I thought you said she was from England.

MABLE: England? Not a bit of it. Liz is a child of the prairie. Aren't you, Liz?

(LIZ *nods, keeps weeping.*)

Willa Cather. John Deere tractors. Tornado insurance.

ROSCOE: Oh—I thought you said northern England somewhere.

MABLE: Get the wax out of your ears, Roscoe. Listen up!

(*Sudden silence except for* LIZ, *now softly weeping. This lasts for a while.*)

(*To* ROSCOE.) You see what you miss when you don't listen? When you have something always on your mind?

(ROSCOE'*s attention is completely on* LIZ *while* MABLE *seems to be listening to the space at large.* ROSCOE *moves slowly toward* LIZ, *who keeps crying, head down, hands in her lap. He stops next to* LIZ *and starts to put his hand on her shoulder.*)

ROSCOE: (*To* LIZ.) Miss?

MABLE: Don't touch her!

(ROSCOE *snaps his hand back but stays by* LIZ, *who continues softly crying.*)

She'll get over it. Always does. That's the thing about these pioneer types. The ability to spring back in the face of terrible adversity. That's not part of your character, though, is it, Mr. Hubbard? Resilience.

ROSCOE: I just don't think there's any reason to humiliate someone like that.

MABLE: Reason? You're looking for a reason? (*Pause as she studies him.*) You'd crumble at the drop of a hat, wouldn't you, Roscoe? Fragile as a skinny wafer. (*Pause.*) Liz, wheel me up to the edge there; my lookout spot. I'd like to gaze out into the abyss for a while.

(LIZ *immediately quits crying—stands—obediently crosses to* MABLE's *wheelchair, releases hand brake, and pushes* MABLE *extreme down left, then out onto the elevated cliff, stopping at the very edge.* MABLE *stares out over the vast valley of Los Angeles,* LIZ *standing dutifully behind her, now fully in control of her emotions. They have left* ROSCOE *alone, standing by the table. Pause.*)

(*Staring out over audience.*) Frightening, isn't it?

ROSCOE: (*Looking out, but staying by table.*) Sally told me there's too much smog today to see the ocean. Even though it's blue.

MABLE: (*Staring out.*) What's blue?

ROSCOE: The smog.

MABLE: Blue smog? Who told you that nonsense?

ROSCOE: Sally. Your daughter.

MABLE: I know who Sally is. Do you?

ROSCOE: Well—for just a short time—

MABLE: Did she tell you about herself? Her scar?

ROSCOE: Scar?

MABLE: Don't tell me you haven't noticed. I'm sure you've encountered it firsthand.

ROSCOE: Well, I—

MABLE: Studied it closely in the gleaming moonlight.

ROSCOE: Me and Sally are just—

MABLE: "Friends"—yes. You told me.

ROSCOE: All she said was—

MABLE: Surgery. "Aortic incompetence" is how they put it. Like a demented child. Leakage of blood back into the left ventricle. Failure of the valve to close properly.

ROSCOE: Oh, no. She never told me it was that serious.

MABLE: Odd, isn't it? How something can be slowly seeping like that—drop by drop. No sign of its dogged devastation. Just dripping away. Invisible.

ROSCOE: How old was she when she had the—

MABLE: A baby, really. Ten—or something. Imagine—at the threshold so early. (*Pause.*) A donor appeared.

(LIZ *turns her back to audience and holds one hand to her face.*)

A miracle. Young girl. Same age. Out of nowhere. Murder victim, they said. Slaughtered in her own backyard, playing with dolls in the sand. Never found the killer. (*Pause.*) Sally was on the list—they have a list for hearts, you know. You have to wait for one to appear. Car wrecks. Suicides. You have to wait. Sally was next in line. The girl's heart was flown across the country in a glass box, surrounded by dry ice—floating in fog. Handled with blue plastic gloves. White masks. Shoes covered in cotton. Sally's dripping heart was taken out. Handed from hand to hand. Her blood contained . . . (*Continuing.*) . . . in a tank. My pink daughter—just a corpse waiting to be brought back to life. No breath. No mind. Sliced open like a deer in the woods. Steaming in the yellow leaves. Dead to this world.

(*Light begins to fade on* MABLE, LIZ, *and* ROSCOE. *Extreme down right, on the very edge of stage,* SALLY *appears in a yellow spot and sings directly to audience as other characters fade to black.*)

SALLY: (*Singing sweetly.*)
  I want to stay alive
  I want to stay alive
  How many times
  I catch myself
  I want to stay alive.

(SALLY, *alone in spot, fades to black.*)

Act Two

In the dark, LIZ's *voice, which we've never heard until now, starts singing refrain from song. Light and sweet— somewhere near* ROSCOE's *bed, right of center.*

LIZ's VOICE: (*In dark.*)
I'm slipping out of time
Falling in my mind
Ten thousand times I catch myself
I'm watching what is mine.

From end of song refrain LIZ's *voice shifts into heavy breathing and moaning, moving into sounds of full-blown sex as lights slowly rise.* LIZ *is mounted on top of* ROSCOE, *her pale back to audience.* ROSCOE *makes occasional, reluctant groans.* LIZ *still has her nurse's skirt on, hiked up to her thighs. Her blouse is down around her waist, but she wears a white bra. She keeps her nurse's cap on. Her white stockings are draped over the foot of the bed and her white, short-heeled shoes are neatly side by side beneath stockings. As* LIZ *arrives at the summit of her climax,* SALLY, *who is fully dressed in pajama bottoms and blouse, emerges out of darkness upstage left, camera mounted on her shoulder, eye to lens, taping* LIZ *and* ROSCOE *in action.* LIZ *leaps off* ROSCOE *when she realizes* SALLY'*s presence. When* LIZ *turns toward audience, desperately pulling her skirt down and her blouse up, the same long, snaking pink scar as* SALLY'*s is revealed on* LIZ'*s chest. This should be such a sudden visual flash that the audience wonders if they're seeing things.* LIZ *grabs her stockings and shoes, rushes off stage right, leaving* ROSCOE *spread-eagled on bed in his underwear, trying to catch his breath.* SALLY *keeps right on shooting* ROSCOE, *getting tighter on him.*

ROSCOE: (*Sitting up.*) Oh my God. What do you think you're doing?

SALLY: (*Still shooting.*) Recording raw life.

ROSCOE: Don't be stupid! This is not a porn movie!

SALLY: It is what it is.

(ROSCOE *groans, lies back down, rolls over with his back to* SALLY, *wrapping himself up in sheet.* SALLY *keeps shooting.*)

ROSCOE: You sound like some fifties jazz hipster. Go away!

SALLY: (*Climbing up on foot of bed, shooting down on* ROSCOE.) Be nice. This is just a tiny piece of the total picture.

ROSCOE: What "total picture"! There is no "total picture"! All you've got is a bunch of fractured footage!

SALLY: (*Still shooting.*) We don't call it "footage" anymore, Professor.

ROSCOE: "Gigabytes"—flash memory—or whatever. Just get out of here! What's the matter with you?

SALLY: (*Shooting.*) Tell us something about your fabulous allure, Professor. At your age. How is it possible—

ROSCOE: She's supposed to be mute, isn't she!

SALLY: (*Eye to lens.*) Could've fooled me.

ROSCOE: Everything about this woman is suspicious. First she's from England, then, suddenly, she's from Nebraska. What's going on?

SALLY: My mother dug her up. I don't know.

ROSCOE: This is beyond belief!

SALLY: It is kinda, isn't it? It's going to make a great segue between your interviews on Borges and Cervantes, though.

ROSCOE: (*Sitting up violently.*) Turn that thing off! (*Pushes* SALLY *off the bed.*) You're not using any of that footage or what—

SALLY: Most men wouldn't complain.

ROSCOE: I'm married!

(*Pause.*)

SALLY: Oh— (*Lowering camera, keeps her balance.*)

ROSCOE: I mean—I still think of myself as—

SALLY: I didn't realize you still—

ROSCOE: I mean—except for you and me—of course.

SALLY: When you must've temporarily lost your mind.

(*Long pause while* SALLY *puts camera and equipment back under her bed and* ROSCOE *sits on edge of his bed.*)

ROSCOE: I don't know what I'm doing here.

(LUCY *suddenly enters from down right with tray and empty syringes. She stops.* ROSCOE *abruptly stands and starts getting dressed.*)

LUCY: Oh—sorry—am I interrupting something?

SALLY: (*To* LUCY.) Performed your duties already?

LUCY: (*Referring to* MABLE.) She's feeling no pain.

SALLY: Attagirl.

LUCY: (*To* SALLY.) Have you seen Elizabeth?

(ROSCOE *gives a quick look to* SALLY, *continues dressing.* SALLY *smiles at* LUCY.)

SALLY: (*To* LUCY.) No, I haven't. She's not with Mable?

LUCY: (*Crossing to table, setting tray down.*) No sign of her. She's usually perched by Mother's bedside this time of morning, doing her nails in some somber color. (*Short pause.*) Any coffee?

ROSCOE: Uh—no—we didn't—

SALLY: (*Smiles at* LUCY.) Too busy.

LUCY: Busy? I thought you two had nothing to do but interview each other.

ROSCOE: (*Abruptly, to* LUCY.) Where did this woman come from?

LUCY: Who?

ROSCOE: This—nurse. This—

LUCY: Oh, Elizabeth? Just showed up out of the blue.

ROSCOE: Just appeared?

LUCY: Mother needed constant attention after her accident. Why?

ROSCOE: I don't know. She just seems—out of place. I mean—

LUCY: Really? I was going to say the same about you, Roscoe.

ROSCOE: What's that?

LUCY: "Out of place."

SALLY: (*To* ROSCOE.) Rudeness runs in a direct line, down from the mother.

LUCY: I mean, what are you doing here exactly, Roscoe?

ROSCOE: I'm just—

SALLY: He's hanging out with me.

LUCY: "Hanging out"? Like teenagers or something?

ROSCOE: No—I mean—Sally helped me after this blowup with my wife.

LUCY: She did? She soothed you? Made it all better?

SALLY: (*Calmly.*) Fuck you, Lucy.

ROSCOE: This thing happened—this schism. I didn't see it coming. In a moment everything comes unraveled. Years and years—kids—schools—peanut butter sandwiches—then—your whole life turns upside down. Just like that. It's devastating. Suddenly you're on the road—by yourself—driving—looking for a place to take a shower—

LUCY: Where's your wife now, Roscoe? Your family?

SALLY: (*To* LUCY.) Look—this is none of your business. I asked Roscoe if he wanted to come and stay with us for a while—that's all.

LUCY: Right. You asked Roscoe, but you didn't ask us.

ROSCOE: I can—I can go—I mean—

SALLY: No! You stay here as long as you want. As long as it takes.

ROSCOE: Thanks—I appreciate that but—I don't want to cause any—

(*Gathers up his shoes and socks.*)

SALLY: You're not causing anything, Roscoe. We've always been this way.

(*Awkward pause.*)

ROSCOE: I should walk my dog. I guess—I don't exactly know what to do, tell you the truth. Isn't that terrible? I mean—at my age—to be still so—I didn't see any of this coming. None of it.

(ROSCOE *exits stage right, carrying his shoes and socks.* SALLY *and* LUCY, *left alone with each other. Pause.*)

LUCY: He acts guilty. Like he might be running away from something.

SALLY: What could that be?

LUCY: I don't know, Sally. You invite this total stranger into our house. You know nothing about him, really. He could be —

SALLY: I knew enough about him.

LUCY: What? What do you know? He could be a fleeing felon —

SALLY: He's a highly respected man of letters!

LUCY: You're kidding me. So was the Marquis de Sade!

SALLY: He just needs somewhere to pull himself back together. Give him a break.

LUCY: Don't you find that a little pathetic? Why doesn't he go where he knows people? Friends, family. What's he doing here?

SALLY: He's got no family!

LUCY: Well, he can't have this one!

SALLY: He doesn't want this one! Believe me. (*Pause.*) Why do you care, anyway?

LUCY: I don't, really.

SALLY: You act like you do. (*Pause.*) What difference could it possibly make to you? He's a friend of mine. I like him.

LUCY: That's nice.

SALLY: It is.

(LUCY *sits in stage right chair as the voice of* ROSCOE *is heard offstage right in high falsetto, speaking to his dog again. No sounds from dog.*)

ROSCOE'S VOICE: (*Off right.*) Ready for a walk? What do you think? Walk? Yes? Piss and poop? Let's go. Happy dog—jumping, jumping. Happy, happy. Here we go. Walking, walking. Here we go! Poop and piss. Happy, happy, happy dog—

(ROSCOE's *voice fades, as before. Long pause as* SALLY *sits on her bed, facing audience, staring at floor.* LUCY *fiddles with syringes at table.*)

LUCY: (*Mocking* ROSCOE.) "Happy, happy, happy dog!" (*Pause.*) Have you told him about your heart yet?

SALLY: No, why should I?

LUCY: Just to—

SALLY: Lay all the cards on the table?

LUCY: Well, he must've noticed.

SALLY: What?

LUCY: Your scar.

SALLY: What scar?

LUCY: Oh, Jesus, Sally—didn't he ask about it when you were—

SALLY: I told him I had something stuck in my throat when I was a little kid.

LUCY: Your throat?

SALLY: Yeah.

LUCY: And so they found it necessary to rip your entire torso open from stem to stern?

SALLY: (*Standing violently.*) It kept slipping!

LUCY: What kept slipping?

SALLY: Whatever it was! Deeper and deeper! Every time they'd almost get their fingers on it, whatever it was slipped away!

(*Long pause.* SALLY *just stands there, trembling.* LUCY *remains at table, unable to look at* SALLY.)

LUCY: (*Quietly.*) So—they never found it, then?

SALLY: (*Pause.*) No—they never found it. (*Sits again.*)

LUCY: (*Long pause.*) Why is it—we never talk about this— how come—all this time and we never—

SALLY: What's to talk about?

LUCY: We're sisters!

SALLY: So what? We always have been. We can't help it.

LUCY: I just wonder sometimes.

SALLY: About what?

LUCY: What it must be like.

SALLY: To be a freak, you mean? Walking around with a murdered girl's heart thumping away inside? Some aberration? Is that it? Thinking somehow she—some part of her is still inside me.

LUCY: (*Pause.*) You don't have to hate me, you know. You don't have to feel it's necessary to—

SALLY: This is not my heart! I can't explain to you what it's like. Okay? I can't begin to explain to you what it's like to be—to be—still alive and all the time—all the time knowing—I should be dead!

LUCY: (*Long pause.*) All right. (*Quietly.*) All right.

SALLY: (*Pause.*) Anyway, why would Roscoe want to know all the gory details? What good would it do him? Right now he takes me as I am. Just like I am. That's why I like him. It's as though we just appeared to each other out of nowhere—without any history.

LUCY: Well—

SALLY: What?

LUCY: He should consider himself lucky—a man his age, having someone like you.

SALLY: Like me?

LUCY: So young. So—

SALLY: What?

LUCY: Pretty.

SALLY: Yeah, right—

LUCY: It's true—

SALLY: I don't need flattery from you!

LUCY: I'm not—

SALLY: I just don't want him to know about all this! All right? I don't want him thinking he's involved with some—experiment.

LUCY: No—

SALLY: Before you know it, he'd be picturing it somewhere—the popping ribs—the gushing blood.

LUCY: Sally—

SALLY: Don't tell him!

LUCY: I won't.

SALLY: You might.

LUCY: I'd never do something like that. Why would I do that?

SALLY: Some things just come out without our knowing, don't they? Ancient, burning things. Catastrophes. All in a moment. You're wheeled from the operating room on the stainless steel gurney—you see all their gleaming, beady eyeballs staring down at you. White masks. You hear their excited whispers—the miracle of it! New life! Brought back from the dead by death itself. The pure lucky accident of murder. You're the one! You're the one and only one who deserves to live! Not the poor little empty corpse curled up in the sand. Discarded. Forgotten. Like they've forgotten you were never meant to be living! Never meant to continue breathing. Dead—long, long, long ago. Before the earth began!

(MABLE *suddenly screams from off right.*)

MABLE'S VOICE: (*Off right.*) ELIZABETH!!!!

(LUCY *jumps to her feet as though jolted by lightning. Short pause.*)

LUCY: Why doesn't she ever call *my* name?

(LUCY *goes rushing off, stage right, to attend to* MABLE, *leaving* SALLY *alone. Long pause.* SALLY *just sits on bed—then speaks softly to herself and, again, to some "other."*)

SALLY: (*To herself.*) Oh, boy—here we are again. Just the two of us. Sometimes you think—maybe it will never end.

(*From deep upstage center, suddenly appearing,* LIZ *comes running directly downstage. She is fully clothed except for her white stockings and her shoes, which she carries in her right hand. She is barefoot and her feet are bleeding.* SALLY *stays on bed, unalarmed.* LIZ *stops at glass table, then sits in stage right chair, paying no attention to* SALLY. LIZ *raises her shoes to about head level and then lets them drop to floor. Pause.*)

LIZ: (*Out of breath, without looking toward* SALLY.) You got a rag? Washrag or something.

SALLY: (*Loudly, with finger to lips.*) SHHHHH!!!

LIZ: (*Without turning to* SALLY.) They can't hear us.

SALLY: (*Whispering loudly.*) They might be right around the corner. The whole pack of them.

LIZ: They're all deaf. Deaf and dumb. You know what that's like, don't you? (*Rubbing her feet.*) You got a rag?

(SALLY *gets up, crosses stage right, and exits abruptly.* LIZ, *to* SALLY *offstage, as she picks up one shoe and smells it.*)

You can get it wet if you want to.

(*Sets shoe down, picks up the other one, and runs her hand inside it—pulls out a small leaf, flicks it into the air, and lets it flutter to the floor.*)

Roscoe still out walking his dog?

SALLY: (*Enters from right with wet washrag.*) I guess. He goes off wandering sometimes.

LIZ: Where to?

SALLY: Never says. I assume he's thinking about what he's done.

(SALLY *hands washrag to* LIZ, *then crosses to stage left chair and sits.* LIZ *crosses her legs and begins wiping blood off her toes.*)

LIZ: What *has* he done?

SALLY: You know—abandonment. The wife. The kids. Running away.

LIZ: (*As she cleans her toes.*) They're grown, aren't they? The kids.

SALLY: Yeah. I guess. Still—

LIZ: What?

SALLY: (*Sees* LIZ's *bloody feet. Pause.*) What have you done to your feet, Liz?

LIZ: Running.

SALLY: Barefoot?

LIZ: Can't run in these. (*Holds shoe up.*)

SALLY: Why are you suddenly running? You were never a jogger.

LIZ: There's lots of things you don't know about me.

SALLY: (*Sudden outburst, slams table with her fist.*) Why are you suddenly running!

(LIZ *calmly crosses her legs again and goes on cleaning her other foot with rag. Pause.*)

LIZ: I run when I've come to the end of my rope.

SALLY: Oh—oh, so now what? Now it's time to start running until you bleed! Now it's time to suddenly start talking! Now it's time to start fucking my boyfriend! Is that it?

LIZ: Shh. (*Pause. Calmly.*) I was just experimenting.

SALLY: Experimenting.

LIZ: I was curious.

SALLY: About what?

LIZ: To see if he'd notice.

SALLY: What!

LIZ: (*Pause.*) My—flesh and blood.

SALLY: Didn't look like he was having any trouble with that!

LIZ: My—actuality.

SALLY: Oh— (*Pause.*) Oh, I get it. So I owe you something now?

LIZ: You've always owed me.

SALLY: You've come back to collect, is that it?

LIZ: Don't be melodramatic.

SALLY: I suppose you want your heart back too!

LIZ: (*Long pause.*) If you could, how would you do it?

SALLY: I'd just—do it all in reverse, I suppose. Bring you back to life. That's what you want, isn't it?

LIZ: Then—*you'd* be dead.

SALLY: Yeah.

LIZ: It might not work.

SALLY: No.

LIZ: We'd—both be dead.

SALLY: Yes.

LIZ: Then where would we be?

(*Pause.*)

SALLY: Here—I guess—or—

(*Long pause as* LIZ *slowly turns to* SALLY *and stares at her, then slowly stands, still barefoot.* LIZ *crosses upstage to* SALLY's *bed, kneels down beside it, and pulls out all the camera equipment.* SALLY *stands.*)

SALLY: What are you doing?

(LIZ, *holding all the camera equipment in her arms, walks deliberately back up middle of stage to deep upstage center.* SALLY *makes a move toward* LIZ *as she walks away.*)

What're you doing!

(LIZ *stops deep upstage center where she entered, holds camera high above her head with one arm, and tosses it over the edge upstage. It disappears into the void. Pause then—a very loud crash as though glass windowpanes and metal have collided with concrete from a great height.* SALLY *runs toward* LIZ.)

What the hell have you done to my camera!!

(SALLY *continues to run toward* LIZ, *then stops abruptly when* MABLE, *in wheelchair, and* LUCY, *pushing her, suddenly enter from down right.* LIZ *remains upstage with her back to the rest of them.* LUCY *is very stoned on* MABLE's *drugs.*)

MABLE: (*Sees* LIZ.) Oh, good—she's back. I knew she couldn't stay away from us for very long.

SALLY: (*To* MABLE.) She just threw my camera over the edge!

MABLE: Your what?

SALLY: (*Yelling.*) My life's work!!

MABLE: Maybe now you can get a real job.

(LIZ *turns and walks calmly back downstage past* SALLY *and sits herself back down in stage right chair. She crosses her legs, picks up washrag, and continues cleaning her feet as the rest simply watch her.*)

MABLE: (*To* LIZ.) So, you couldn't get enough of us, huh? (*Pause. Silence from* LIZ.) You're not fooling anyone, sister, you know that, don't you? This silent treatment.

(LIZ *continues cleaning her feet with rag.*)

LUCY: (*Stoned.*) Nothing to say.

SALLY: She threw my camera into the San Fernando Valley.

LUCY: Oh, get over it.

(*Throughout this next scene,* SALLY *works her way to extreme upstage center as though she can't believe she's just lost her life's work, along the same path that* LIZ *took, until she reaches the spot where* LIZ *threw the camera and equipment.*)

MABLE: (*To* LIZ.) I've been onto you all along. Talking to yourself or—whoever it was. Babbling. Screaming in the middle of the night. That was you screaming— wasn't it?

(LIZ *hunches her shoulders, shakes her head, continues cleaning her feet.*)

LUCY: Of course that was you.

MABLE: We've all been onto you, all along. All of us.

SALLY: (*As she crosses upstage.*) Vindictive bitch. Destroy- ing the evidence.

MABLE: (*To* LIZ.) I'm used to treachery and delusion, you know. When Whitmore left me—

LUCY: (*To* LIZ.) That's her husband—

MABLE: (*To* LUCY.) He was *your* father.

LUCY: He's dead.

MABLE: He was still your father.

SALLY: (*Still moving upstage.*) He wasn't *my* father.

MABLE: (*Loudly.*) He was everyone's father! (*Pause.*) Anyway—anyway—don't get me off track here. When Whitmore suddenly went away and abandoned me—

LUCY: (*About* LIZ, *who continues cleaning her feet.*) She's not paying attention.

MABLE: (*Rising in volume.*) When Whitmore went off and left me high and dry! That's when all this began to happen! All this grief! This sudden internal emergency. (*Pause.*) I went away. Where was I? Wisconsin. My summer home. The North Woods, wasn't it? I thought, "This is where I can get ahold of myself."

LUCY: (*To* LIZ.) That's what she thought.

MABLE: Grief is what it was. Grief! Plain and simple. That's what drove me up there.

SALLY: There it is. Down there. I can see it. Smashed to tiny pieces.

(LUCY *rolls* MABLE *to the table next to* LIZ.)

SALLY: Can you hear me?

LUCY: (*To* LIZ.) Now pay attention!

(LUCY *returns to her former place behind* MABLE'S *wheelchair.* LIZ *remains seated, stares at washrag on floor.* MABLE *continues.*)

MABLE: Days went by. Nights. All alone. I'd lay there listening to mice scuttle across the roof. Wind. The loon on the lake.

(*Timing this with* MABLE'S *speech,* SALLY *slowly continues upstage.*)

I'd sometimes walk out there and stare at the moon. I'd wander. Walk toward the little town on washboard roads. See the blue lights of television flicker in people's windows. Middle of the woods. Dogs howling. No cars. Smells of pine and garbage. Dead animals. Bats and owls swooping. I'd keep walking. Listen to my crunching feet. My breath. Not one thought of Whitmore, though. Isn't that remarkable? Not one thought

of him. He'd disappeared completely. Vanished from
my life.

(*Pause.* SALLY *reaches the place where* LIZ *had thrown
her camera and equipment, looks down into the abyss,
then jumps over the edge, upstage, and disappears into
the black. No sound.* LIZ *continues to stare at the rag
on the floor.*)

I walked and walked. I came to the edge of town. No
people. No people that I could see. . . . (*Continuing.*)
Not one. A drive-in movie in the distance. Maybe—I
could just make out the shapes. No voices. No music.
Just forms moving. Bodies. Color. The wind picked
up. I walked straight toward the movie. I kept walking.
As though the movie were pulling me on a string. As
though the forms were speaking. I got closer but still
no sound. I could see the face now. I could clearly see
the face. It was James Dean—lying on his belly in
the red ground. His short sleeves rolled up. I climbed
a tree to get a better look. I got higher and higher. I
could see his black eyebrows twitching. His remarkable eyebrows. He seemed to be talking to somebody
but there was nobody—nothing there but a field of
beans. His lips moved but no voice. He was talking
to the beans. His lips were reaching out to them as
though—as though he were trying to—kiss them or—
caress them—make them grow. His eyes were so—

full of—love. That's all it was. Pure love. I tried to get closer but the whole branch snapped off. I crashed. Rolled in the night. I was broken into a million pieces. Shattered completely.

LUCY: That's when we brought you home.

(*Pause. Suddenly* LIZ *leaps up, grabs the washrag off the floor, returns to her chair, crosses her legs, and goes back to wiping her feet.* LUCY *comes out from behind the wheelchair, very stoned. She approaches* LIZ, *who continues with her feet, silently. To* LIZ, *cautiously.*)

Did you hear anything my mother was saying to you?

(*Her "stonedness" is manifest mostly in a certain heaviness of the head, which now and then results in her nodding off completely, chin on chest, and coming to a standstill, then snapping out of it and continuing. In any case,* LIZ *goes on cleaning her feet and* MABLE *just listens from her wheelchair.*)

Any words at all? She was trying to get something across to you. Imagery—the part about the gravel roads—the crunching—middle of the night—all alone. Any of that stuff? Or—did—did it—did it seem to awaken some—some distant affinity—some recollection—of your own predicament—I mean—your own memory—

what do you call it? Predicament. The—the absence of a voice—for instance—or—or—servitude—

MABLE: Servitude?

LUCY: Maybe—I mean—being at the mercy—more or less—the mercy of— Huh? The mercy of something?

MABLE: Mercy?

LUCY: Maybe nothing. Maybe that's it. Maybe—paralysis.

MABLE: Paralysis?

LUCY: (*To* MABLE.) Well—maybe not that. Maybe—seizure or—

MABLE: Seizure?

LUCY: Well—maybe that's not it either. What I'm trying to say—did it have a certain sort of—resonance—a reverberation—or did it just go in one ear and out the other. That's what I'm trying to get at.

MABLE: (*To* LIZ.) My daughter has been dipping into my medications. You'll have to excuse her, Liz.

LUCY: That's not the case—that's not the case at all.

MABLE: Remarkable, how we can't face what's right in front of us.

LUCY: That's simply not the case! I was trying—I was sick of—I mean—sick of taking care of—

MABLE: Me?

LUCY: No, no, no—not *you* so much. I've gotten used to— no—it's me.

MABLE: *You* what?

LUCY: *Me*—in pain.

MABLE: You?

(LIZ *pauses in her cleaning and looks at* LUCY.)

LUCY: Yes.

MABLE: You're not in pain. It's *me*! *Me* that's in pain.

LUCY: No—but sometimes—sometimes I just want—

MABLE: What.

LUCY: Out. Just—

MABLE: Out?

LUCY: Yes.

MABLE: Oh well—maybe—there are times we all could use a little break, I suppose. Isn't that right, Liz?

(LIZ *doesn't answer—goes back to cleaning her feet, then picks up each shoe and carefully cleans the dust from it. Licking and spitting into washrag between wipes.*)

LUCY: I would like to go far, far away.

MABLE: Vacation? Where would you go? Istanbul, or—

LUCY: No. No—somewhere—unheard of.

(LIZ *pauses again and looks at* LUCY.)

MABLE: The wilds of Borneo?

LUCY: No.

MABLE: *I* would like to go to the wilds of Borneo.

(LIZ *returns to her cleaning.*)

LUCY: No—somewhere—without a name. Without definition.

MABLE: Where would that be?

LUCY: Somewhere—unknown.

MABLE: Oh—well—how would you get there if you don't know where you're going?

LUCY: You just—you just—go.

MABLE: You just go? (*Laughs.*) Is this suddenly like Dorothy in Kansas, Liz? Or am I dreaming? Liz?

LUCY: You do. You just—take off.

MABLE: But—how would you find your way?

LUCY: I'd take someone. Someone who could help me.

MABLE: Like Liz? Liz is a great help. Aren't you, Liz? When you're around.

(LIZ *looks again at* LUCY.)

LUCY: Liz is with *you*.

MABLE: Yes, she is.

LUCY: Well—she can't go with me, then, if she's with you.

MABLE: No. No, she can't. I was just using her as an example.

LIZ: (*Singing.*)
If they could only hear me now

(LIZ *turns back to her cleaning. Sound of* SALLY's *voice, screaming wildly—*ROSCOE *responding.*)

SALLY'S VOICE: (*Yelling, off right.*) NO! YOU CAN'T GO! YOU CAN'T GO NOW!

ROSCOE'S VOICE: (*Loudly, off right.*) Let go, Sally! I'm telling you! Let go!

SALLY'S VOICE: NO! YOU CAN'T JUST RUN OFF AND LEAVE ME!

(*From stage right,* ROSCOE *and* SALLY *enter—*ROSCOE *pulling* SALLY *onstage in great heaves.* SALLY *has a hold on the grip of an old-fashioned suitcase—yellow with leather trim—*ROSCOE *pulling her, holding both sides*

of suitcase and yanking her along. He works his way
backward toward his bed.)

ROSCOE: (*Pulling.*) I've had enough of this! Really. Everyone's tired of me being here. I'm tired of me being
here. You're tired of me being here!

SALLY: (*Pulling hard against him.*) I'm not! I'm not tired
of you! I'm not!

(*Suddenly the handle of the suitcase breaks away and*
SALLY *goes tumbling backward*—ROSCOE *goes tum-*
bling the opposite way, holding on to the suitcase—*they*
both fall—*in the manner of the old vaudeville pratfall.*
SALLY *remains on the floor, on her back, holding the*
grip of the suitcase high above her chest, and begins
weeping loudly. ROSCOE *gathers himself together; takes*
suitcase to his bed and set it down on top of bed; opens
it, kneels down beside bed, and starts taking items out
from under bed like shirts, books, underwear, socks, and
throwing them in suitcase. LUCY *slowly goes over to*
SALLY *and just stands, looking down at her, as* SALLY
continues weeping on floor. ROSCOE, *wildly packing.*
MABLE *watches from her wheelchair.*)

ROSCOE: (*Packing items.*) I've had enough of this. This
is just—I can't—I can't just continue hanging on here
as though—as though—something were going to

appear—as though something were going to happen out of the blue, suddenly—and—and—make everything go away or—or—correct things—or—change—or—save me.

SALLY: (*Still on back, sobbing, holding suitcase grip in both hands.*) WE WERE GOING TO FALL IN LOVE!

ROSCOE: (*Continuing to pack.*) No! No, we weren't! No, we weren't at all! That's just—that's not part of—I was just in limbo—that's all. Love is—love was never—

SALLY: You said—you told me—

ROSCOE: No, no. You're mistaken! I never told you anything!

SALLY: YOU DID! YOU TOLD ME! We were on the verge of something.

LUCY: (*Stoned.*) This is so fucked-up.

MABLE: Aw, let them play it out. They'll get over it. We all get over it one way or the other.

SALLY: (*Continues weeping.*) You told me we would—you said—

ROSCOE: (*Packing furiously.*) No! No, no, no, no, no! I never promised you anything! I never—

SALLY: (*Still on her back.*) How can you lie to me like that? To my face! You said I was the one! I was the one and only one!

(LIZ *suddenly stands, throws washrag on ground, walks over to* ROSCOE's *bed, picks up his suitcase, and dumps all the contents on the floor, throws suitcase down, then returns to her chair, picks up washrag, and goes on cleaning her shoes.* SALLY *stops crying, lowers her arms, sits up, and looks toward suitcase.*)

ROSCOE: (*Pause. To* LIZ, *who ignores him.*) What was that! What was that for? (*Picks up his suitcase and starts throwing all his items back into it.*) I've never seen such a house full of wackos! This is—this is just— What's the matter with you people?

MABLE: Oh, now he's turning against us. He was full of gratitude before. Full of humility. Now—

(LUCY *moves toward* ROSCOE, *who's packing desperately.*)

LUCY: (*Still stoned, to* ROSCOE.) Are you—are you feeling uncomfortable, Roscoe? With us—I mean have you reached—have you reached saturation point?

ROSCOE: (*Still packing.*) Just don't—don't—let me get this done and get out of here! Please. That's all I'm asking.

LUCY: You're hitting the road? Is that it?

ROSCOE: That's it! That's exactly it!

MABLE: Back to the little lady! Back to the wife and kiddies?

ROSCOE: Not necessarily, no!

SALLY: Necessarily?

ROSCOE: I mean—

LUCY: What kind of car do you have?

ROSCOE: (*Pauses in his packing.*) What?

LUCY: What kind of car?

ROSCOE: (*Continues packing.*) What's that got to do with it?

LUCY: So I can picture it.

MABLE: She needs pictures.

ROSCOE: It's a Chevy, for Christ's sake!

MABLE: A Chevy!

(LUCY *suddenly steps in, picks up* ROSCOE's *suitcase, and dumps contents on the floor, then throws the suitcase down.* ROSCOE *just stands there in disbelief.* MABLE *suddenly singing.*)

MABLE: *See the USA*
In your Chevrolet
America is asking
You to call

Drive your Chevrolet
Through the USA
America's the greatest
land of all

SALLY: (*Still sitting on floor.*) See, Lucy even wants you to stay. (ROSCOE *starts shaking his head side to side, which turns into a kind of spasmodic mannerism, as though he's on the brink of a nervous breakdown.*)

(ROSCOE *picks up all the dumped items on the floor— carries them to the bed—dumps them in a pile—goes to suitcase, throws it on bed, and starts to repack; all the while he keeps his head going while beginning to emit a high, desperate squealing sound.*)

ROSCOE: (*Throwing things in suitcase.*) No! No, she doesn't! She's the one—she's the one who got me thinking about this whole thing. "Out of place," she said! That's what she called me. "Out of place"!

LUCY: I was only joking.

MABLE: She's the joker.

LUCY: I'm always joking.

ROSCOE: No! No, no, no! I'm out of here! I'm so far out of here—

SALLY: (*On floor.*) Where are you going to go, Roscoe? Have you thought about that?

ROSCOE: (*Packing and twitching desperately.*) Of course I've thought about that! Of course! You don't think I'd just—I'd just take off out of here without a plan—a destination—do you? Is that what you think?

MABLE: We don't know what to think.

LUCY: You're a mess, Roscoe.

ROSCOE: I'm a mess? *I'm* a mess?

SALLY: You won't get very far. I can tell. You'll break down somewhere.

MABLE: Yes. You're headed for a very serious breakdown, young man.

ROSCOE: (*Throwing things in suitcase.*) I'm not young! I'm not young anymore!

LUCY: I'll say.

(*Throughout all of this,* LIZ *continues calmly and silently cleaning her shoes in the down right chair.*)

ROSCOE: (*To* LUCY.) Shut up!

MABLE: (*To* SALLY.) Can't handle the truth. That's the major part of it.

SALLY: The truth is—he never loved me. I can see that now.

ROSCOE: I did—at one point in time—

SALLY: Ha!

(SALLY *stands. Brushes herself off.*)

ROSCOE: I did! I absolutely did! I can tell—I can tell when I'm feeling something. When something—

SALLY: What?

ROSCOE: Happens—you know.

SALLY: When something happens?

ROSCOE: When something begins to take place—take shape.

(SALLY *walks directly over to* ROSCOE's *bed and dumps suitcase just like the others.*)

(*Screaming.*) NO!! Oh God. Oh my God!

MABLE: God won't help you now.

ROSCOE: What have I done? (*Holds his head with both hands to stop the shaking.*) WHAT HAVE I DONE!! Why me? What have I done to you people? I'm just a visitor here. I haven't done anything. I'm totally innocent.

(SALLY *crosses calmly to her bed, stage left; lies down on it, hands behind her head, staring at ceiling.* ROSCOE *collapses, sitting down on his bed in the midst of the pile of items and open suitcase. He starts rocking back and forth, holding his head with both hands, like a madman about to erupt into a seizure.* LUCY *stands there, watching him sympathetically.* MABLE *just watches from her wheelchair and* LIZ *goes on calmly cleaning her shoes, spitting and licking rag.*)

LUCY: (*Sweetly—going to* ROSCOE.) You've messed up, Roscoe. You have to realize that. You have to swallow it. Digest it. You've really fucked up.

ROSCOE: (*Rocking violently on bed.*) NO!! NO!!

LUCY: (*Sitting down beside* ROSCOE, *patting his back as he rocks.*) Yes. Running away is a cowardly act. There's nothing else to be said about it.

ROSCOE: (*Rocking.*) I didn't! It was over! That's all it was. Over! Over, over, over, over! What's the point—what's the point in continuing?

SALLY: (*Lying on her back on bed.*) Well—you'll be all right once you hit the road.

MABLE: That's right. You'd be amazed how a Dairy Queen will change your entire attitude.

ROSCOE: NO! No, no, no, no, no!

SALLY: The open road.

MABLE: (*Singing.*)
See the USA in your
Chevrolet
The Rockies way out west

ROSCOE: I don't want to go!
I don't want to go!

SALLY: (*Still lying down.*)
I thought you said—

Are calling you

ROSCOE: (*Rocking desperately.*) There's
nothing out there!
Miles and miles and
miles— Nothing!
Absolutely nothing!

Drive your Chevrolet

Through the USA

Where fields of golden
wheat

LUCY: But once you've got
that big engine
running—

pass in review

ROSCOE: NOTHING! Empty—nothing moves. Broken
towns. Tractors rusted out. Wichita—Topeka.

LUCY: I can drive for you if you want. You can sleep in the
back. I love to drive.

ROSCOE: No! I can't—I can't—

SALLY: (*Still on her back.*) Well, you can't stay here anymore.

(ROSCOE *stands—*SALLY's *line has brought him round suddenly.*)

ROSCOE: (*Standing.*) No—of course. Of course not.

MABLE: You'll have to find other digs, Roscoe.

ROSCOE: Yes. Of course I do—of course. I understand that.

(ROSCOE *starts again, making feeble attempts to pack his suitcase.* LUCY *stands and watches him.*)

LUCY: Why don't you give me the keys and I'll go warm that Chevy up for you.

ROSCOE: (*Packing.*) No—I—can do it. I mean—

SALLY: She's a good driver, Roscoe.

ROSCOE: No—I can drive myself. I've always done my own driving. Always. Ever since I was a little boy. Driving. I drove everywhere. (*As he packs.*) I drove away from— I was always—always on the move. Running—I mean. Gunning the engine. Racing through orchards and—

they never caught me. Never once. I was so—they couldn't believe how I'd disappear. Right under their noses. Vanish. Squealing. Like a demon. Bullets ripping all around me. Fires. Slashing wind. Sirens and flashlights. Hounds. Still they couldn't bring me down! Couldn't catch me. I left no signs. No trace. A phantom. That's what it was. A ghost. I'd . . . (*Continuing as he frantically packs suitcase.*) . . . disappear. Turn up in another county. Different time. They'd send radio cars—vigilantes. Ropes and rifles. Tear gas—hand grenades. Bottles of butane. Fires swept through the countryside, trying to smoke me out. Fires burning day and night. Raging through the foothills. Animals fled. Smoke. Men. Horseback. Posses. Torches. It was—it was— (*Still trying to pack his things, going in circles.*) They laid siege to the— Freeways crumbled! The watershed! Floods and—floods and—dust and—wind all blasts of— All the canaries died!

(*He stops. Comes to a standstill. Looks around at the others as though he's just realized where he is in space and time. Suddenly everyone stops—even* LIZ *stops her obsessive cleaning. It's as though they are all intensely listening to something that can't be heard. This is not a "freeze" exercise or a stylized tableau but a real moment in time where everyone just listens silently. The moment lasts for a while; then* LUCY *steps up to* ROSCOE, *stops directly in front of him, and holds out an open palm to him.*)

LUCY: (*To* ROSCOE.) Keys.

(ROSCOE *pauses, then digs around in his pocket and pulls out the keys to the Chevy. He hands them to her.*)

I'll pull it up in the driveway.

(ROSCOE *nods.* LUCY *exits right with keys. From this point on,* LIZ *sits silently, very still, facing out toward audience, both feet on floor, hands on knees, back very straight, no movement.*)

MABLE: She's an excellent driver, Roscoe. She can drive till the cows come home.

SALLY: She's a little bit stoned, don't you think?

MABLE: She'll pull out of that somewhere around the Grapevine. You're headed out that direction, aren't you, Roscoe? San Bernardino, Cucamonga, out through Arizona?

ROSCOE: (*Still standing, bewildered.*) I—

MABLE: That's the way I'd go if I were you. If I were heading east. Barstow, Yermo, Ludlow, Needles. That's the route I'd take. Stop along the way. Enjoy the sights. Plenty a stuff to see.

SALLY: (*Sitting up on her bed.*) She might have a head-on collision, in the condition she's in.

MABLE: Stop and see Trigger in Victorville. Roy Rogers's horse. You remember Trigger, don't you? They got him stuffed right there in a museum. Right by the side of the road.

SALLY: (*Sitting on her bed.*) I think they sold Trigger.

MABLE: Naw, naw—they wouldn't have sold Trigger. He's a national treasure—a monument. Everyone remembers Trigger. Why would they sell him?

SALLY: Worms and moths—stuffing coming out of him.

MABLE: Worms and moths?

SALLY: I think they auctioned him off, actually.

MABLE: That's impossible! Who would have bought him?

SALLY: I think some rich guy from England.

MABLE: England? England again! They never did have any respect for our true moral fiber. The absolute arrogance—England!

SALLY: I could be wrong.

MABLE: I think so. I think you must be. Something like
that wouldn't pass us by unnoticed. They'd have a citi-
zen's alert, wouldn't they? It would cause an uproar,
something like that. Selling Trigger—the very idea—

SALLY: I must be wrong.

MABLE: You must be! It's irresponsible—a statement
like that.

SALLY: I'm sorry.

MABLE: You have to learn to think before you speak.

SALLY: I'm sorry.

MABLE: You can't just say any old thing that comes into
your head.

SALLY: No.

MABLE: Where would we be—where would that leave us
if everything went on like that? Random—chaotic—

SALLY: I'm very sorry.

(ROSCOE *just stands there in a daze, watching* MABLE
and SALLY. LIZ *continues to sit in chair, very still, looking out. The Chevy car horn suddenly blasts for about*

*five full seconds, off right. Everything stops. Then
silence. The dog starts barking, off right, and continues
intermittently through the end of play. This is the first
time we've heard the dog.* ROSCOE *starts to exit toward
the car horn, almost robotically.* SALLY *stops him.*)

What about your things?

(ROSCOE *stops, turns toward suitcases, then looks at*
SALLY.)

ROSCOE: I don't need them.

SALLY: What about a change of clothes? Toothbrush.

ROSCOE: I don't need them.

SALLY: What about me?

(ROSCOE *looks at her awhile, then turns and starts to
exit right again.* SALLY *stops him. Dog keeps barking
through this.*)

You know what's going to happen don't you?

(ROSCOE *stops but keeps his back to her.*)

You're just going to get more and more lost. She's not
going to take you anywhere. You don't even know

where you're going, do you? The two of you. What a pair. Wandering. You don't even have a map I'll bet. Do you? I bet you don't even have a map.

(*Pause.* ROSCOE *exits right, never turning to look at* SALLY, *who just stands there watching him leave. Dog continues barking.* MABLE *watches from wheelchair.* LIZ *sits there motionless, facing audience. Offstage, sounds of car door slamming shut, Chevy driving away. Silence. Dog barks.*)

MABLE: Sally, take me up to my lookout spot. Take me up there.

(SALLY *goes to the wheelchair, pushes* MABLE *stage left and out onto lookout ramp. She stops wheelchair at very edge of ramp and stays with* MABLE. *Pause. Dog keeps barking off and on.* LIZ *remains still.* MABLE *looks out over audience to L.A.*)

He's forgot his dog.

SALLY: Sounds like it.

MABLE: Now we're stuck with it.

SALLY: Yeah. (*Pause.*) We could turn it loose.

MABLE: Coyotes would get it.

SALLY: Yeah.

(*Pause.*)

MABLE: We could shoot it.

SALLY: Yeah.

MABLE: Dump it over the edge.

SALLY: Probably start stinking, though.

MABLE: Yeah.

SALLY: Neighbors would get alarmed. Murder or something.

MABLE: Drug retribution.

(*Pause.*)

SALLY: Do dogs smell like humans?

MABLE: When they're dead, you mean?

SALLY: Yeah.

MABLE: Sweeter, maybe.

SALLY: Sweeter?

MABLE: Maybe.

SALLY: Like dried blood, you mean?

MABLE: Like—death. You know.

SALLY: Then we all smell alike, I guess. Dogs and humans.

MABLE: There must be some difference.

SALLY: What is it?

MABLE: What?

SALLY: The difference.

(*Long pause. Nothing happens.*)

Mom?

MABLE: What?

SALLY: How come you saved me when you knew I was doomed? When you knew it was hopeless. How come you kept me going?

(*Pause.*)

MABLE: What are mothers for?

(LIZ *starts singing. Very simple. No accompaniment. Lights start fading very slowly as* MABLE *and* SALLY *just stand there.*)

LIZ: (A *capella.*)
I want to come to life
I do
I do
I want to come alive
I do
I do
This swimming in the dark
Is tearing me apart
I want to come to life
I do
I do.

(*Dog keeps barking intermittently as lights fade slowly to black. Lights up for curtain call. After first bow, "Choctaw Bingo" by James McMurtry comes on loud and clear and continues as audience leaves the house. The barking dog is drowned out, but if the song ends before the last member of the audience has left, the dog comes back—in the distance.*)